P9-DBO-446

I WONDER Why

The Sun Rises

and other questions about time and seasons

Brenda Walpole

KINGFISHER

NEW YORK

Copyright © 2011 by Kingfisher
Published in the United States by Kingfisher
175 Fifth Ave., New York, NY 10010
Kingfisher is an imprint of
Macmillan Children's Books, London.
All rights reserved.

First published in 1996 by Kingfisher
This edition published 2011 by Kingfisher

Distributed in the U.S. by Macmillan, 175 Fifth Ave.,
New York, NY 10010
Distributed in Canada by H.B. Fenn and Company Ltd.,
34 Nixon Road, Bolton, Ontario L7E 1W2

Library of Congress Cataloging-in-Publication data
has been applied for.

ISBN 978-0-7534-6561-5 (HC)
ISBN 978-0-7534-6529-5 (PB)

Kingfisher books are available for special promotions and
premiums. For details contact: Special Markets Department,
Macmillan, 175 Fifth Avenue, New York, NY 10010.

For more information, please visit
www.kingfisherbooks.com

Printed in China
9 8 7 6 5 4 3 2 1
1TR/1010/WKT/UTD/140MA

Consultant: Ian Graham
Illustrations: Susanna Addario 10-11; Peter Dennis (Linda
    Rogers) 4-5; Chris Forsey cover, 6-7, 20-21; Terry Gabbey
    (AFA Ltd) 16-17, 24-25; Craig Greenwood (Wildlife Art
    Agency) 12-13; Christian Hook 26-27; Biz Hull (Artist
    Partners) 14-15, 22-23, 30-31; Tony Kenyon (BL Kearley)
    all cartoons; Nicki Palin 18-19; Ian Thompson 8-9, 28-29.

CONTENTS

Why does the Sun rise in the morning?

Every morning, the Sun rises in the east. Its light wakes animals early. A new day begins.

The Sun doesn't actually rise at all! It's Earth that turns around to give us a sunrise each morning. Earth is like a spinning ball. Wherever you are, it starts to get light as your part of Earth spins around to face the Sun. The sky grows brighter and it is morning.

The ancient Greeks believed that the Sun was a god named Helios. He rode across the sky in a chariot of flames.

The weather may be gray and gloomy, but above the clouds, the Sun is always shining.

4

Why does it get dark at night?

Earth keeps spinning all day long. As it moves, the Sun seems to travel across the sky. As the hours pass, your part of Earth turns farther away from the Sun. The Sun seems to sink in the sky and darkness comes. It is night.

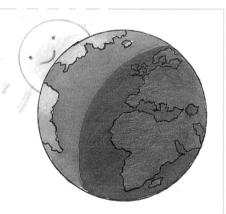

It takes 24 hours for Earth to turn around once. While one half has daylight, the other half has night.

At night, one side of Earth is in deep shadow. This makes it feel much cooler, so you often need to wrap up warm.

Where is it night all day long?

During the winter months, the lands around the poles don't see the Sun at all. The Sun is so low in the sky that it's hidden below the horizon. This makes the days cold and dark— even at noon.

After the dark days of winter, it is wonderful to see the Sun again. The Inuit people of North America used to celebrate its return by lighting new lamps in their homes.

During the summer, it is very different at the poles. The Sun is in the sky morning, noon, and night. For the seals, it must be like sleeping with the lights on.

Winter days are dark in the northern lands of Scandinavia. Sami, or Lapp, children go to school by the light of the Moon and stars.

Some people are so miserable in the dark days of winter that they get sick. Doctors call this seasonal affective disorder (SAD) and find that special types of bright lights often cheer up their patients.

Where do all the days start on time?

In tropical lands near the equator, the Sun rises at almost the same time every morning. And it sets at almost the same time every evening! The days and nights are each about 12 hours long—every single day of the year.

Why do we have seasons?

We have seasons because of the way Earth spins around, or orbits, the Sun. Each orbit takes one year from start to finish. Earth is tilted, and as the planet orbits, first one pole and then the other leans toward the Sun. This is what gives us the seasons.

4. In September, neither pole leans toward the Sun. There is fall in the north and spring in the south.

N

4

S

N

1

S

1. In December, the North Pole leans away from the Sun. The northern half of Earth has winter. The southern half has summer.

Earth spins around as it orbits the Sun. It doesn't spin upright, however, but tilts to one side.

  The seasons are different in the northern and southern halves of Earth. Depending on where you are, wearing a swimsuit in December could give you frostbite or a sunburn!

3. In June, the North Pole leans toward the Sun. The northern half of Earth has summer. The southern half has winter.

N

③

N

S

②

The weather is always hot at the equator because the Sun is high overhead. But at the poles, the Sun is lower in the sky. Its rays are spread out and feel much weaker.

2. In March, neither pole leans toward the Sun. There is spring in the north and fall in the south.

9

Why do we plant seeds in the spring?

Seeds need to be warm and wet before they can sprout. As the spring sunshine starts to warm the ground, farmers and gardeners dig the soil and sow their seeds. The plants don't take long to grow.

Bees can see patterns and colors on flower petals that we can't see. They guide them in like landing lights on an airport runway.

Why are bees busy in the summer?

On warm, sunny days, bees are busy visiting hundreds of flowers. Inside each flower is a drop of sugar-sweet nectar. Bees feed on it and use it to make honey back at their hive.

Why do leaves drop in the fall?

In the fall, trees find it difficult to suck up water from the cold, frozen ground, so their leaves dry out. The leaves turn red, gold, and brown and drop to the ground, leaving the trees bare for the winter. The trees will grow new leaves in the spring.

Not all trees lose their leaves. Conifers have tough leaves that can survive the winter cold.

Why do animals sleep through the winter?

For some animals, sleeping is the best way to survive the hungry winter days. Chipmunks, squirrels, hedgehogs, and some bears eat as much as they can in the fall and then sleep somewhere safe until the spring.

Many animals grow thick winter coats to help them survive the bitter cold.

11

Where are there only two seasons?

Many tropical countries have only two seasons every year. One is very wet, and the other is very dry. Not many trees manage to survive the dry months, and animals travel hundreds of miles searching for food and water.

Many animals migrate in different seasons. Every year, swarms of monarch butterflies leave Mexico and fly 1,860 miles (3,000km) to spend the summer by cool Canadian lakes.

During the dry season, the ground is baked hard by the hot sun. Clouds of dust cover everything and everyone.

In the dry season, herds of wildebeests and zebras cross the grasslands of central Africa. They follow the thunderclouds in search of rainwater and fresh grass.

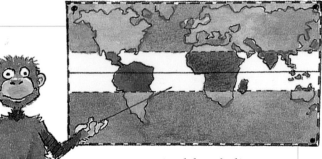

Tropical lands lie near the equator. They are the warmest parts of Earth.

Where does it pour for a month?

Some parts of India and Southeast Asia have long, heavy downpours called monsoons. Big black clouds are blown in from the sea during the summer months. Once the rain starts, it can last for weeks, flooding fields and streets.

Who can tell time without a clock?

We all can! Inside every one of us there's something called a body clock. It wakes us up every morning and tells us that it's breakfast time. And throughout the day, we seem to know just when it's time to work, eat, and play. As evening comes, we feel tired and get ready to sleep.

Newborn babies don't know their days from their nights. They just wake up their parents whenever they feel hungry!

Different kinds of animals live to different kinds of clocks. A bee and a badger never meet. One is active by day, while the other is active at night.

14

Can flowers tell time?

A few flowers are such good timekeepers that they open at the same time every day. Gardeners sometimes plant flowers like these in flower clocks. There are as many as 12 different flowers in one "clock," and they open one after the other as the hours pass.

Animals have body clocks, too. In zoos and on farms, many of them know when it's feeding time.

Can animals tell time?

Some wild animals are active by day, and others wake up only at night. They can't tell the time of day or night, but some animals do know the time of year. The Canadian snowshoe hare knows when winter's coming. It grows a white fur coat to hide from foxes when the snow arrives.

Which calendar was carved in stone?

Many hundreds of years ago, people called the Aztecs lived in Central America. They made a calendar from a huge stone shaped like the Sun. The face of the Sun god was carved in the middle, and signs for the days were carved all around the edge.

Who invented our calendar?

More than 2,000 years ago, a Roman ruler named Julius Caesar invented the calendar that we use today. He gave each year 365 days and arranged them in 12 months. Since then, the calendar has hardly changed.

The Aztec calendar stone measured almost 13 feet (4m) from side to side—that's far too big to hang on a wall!

What is a leap year?

Every four years we have what we call a leap year. This is a year with 366 days instead of 365. The extra day is added at the end of February. So if your birthday falls on February 29, it's a very special day indeed.

A leap year can always be divided by four, with none left over. The years 2008, 2012, and 2016 are all leap years.

Why do we need calendars?

Most of us need calendars to help us remember all the things we plan in a year. But they also help us keep track of time. When people are shipwrecked or taken hostage, they find unusual ways to mark the passing days.

17

Who lights lamps at the new year?

The Hindu new year is called the Festival of Light—and no wonder! Towns are strung with lights, and lamps shine from every door and window. The women make beautiful floor pictures with colored chalk, flour, and sand and decorate them with glowing candles.

Chinese new year celebrations can last up to 15 days. They begin between the middle of January and the middle of February.

Who brings in the new year with a bang?

The new year in China starts with beating drums, crashing cymbals, fireworks, and a lion or dragon dancing through the streets. All this noise is supposed to chase away the bad days of the past and bring luck in the future.

There are many Hindu new year festivals. Some occur in the fall, while others are celebrated in the early spring.

On New Year's Eve in Ecuador in South America, people burn the "old year" on a bonfire! It's a figure made from pieces of straw.

Who blows a horn at the new year?

The Jewish new year festival of Rosh Hashanah begins with the blowing of a curved ram's horn. The sound calls people to the synagogue to pray for God's forgiveness for the things they've done wrong in the past year. As the new year begins, they can make a fresh start.

Rosh Hashanah falls in October or November. People eat apples and bread dipped in honey in the hope of a sweet year to come!

How long is a month?

On today's calendars, a month can be as short as 28 days or as long as 31 days. But in the past, a month was the time between one full moon and the next. Every month was exactly the same length, and that was 29.5 days.

The Moon is a dark, lifeless world. It looks bright because one side is always lit up by the Sun. What we call moonlight is actually reflected sunlight.

One piece of music by the German composer Beethoven was nicknamed the "Moonlight Sonata." You can imagine the Moon rising as it plays.

Why does the Moon change shape?

The Moon doesn't really change shape. What changes is the shape of the sunlit part of the Moon that you can see from Earth. As the Moon moves around Earth in its orbit, the Sun lights it from different directions. First the bright side seems to grow, and then it seems to shrink.

The first man on the Moon was Neil Armstrong, an American astronaut who took part in the *Apollo 11* space mission in July 1969.

Who eats the Moon?

Chinese children eat delicious moon-shaped cakes for the Moon-viewing festival. At the September full moon, families walk to the park carrying lanterns. Then they eat their cakes and admire the Moon!

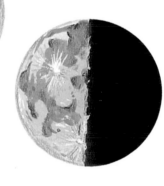

Why are there seven days in a week?

We split the week into workdays and rest days. After five hard days at school, everyone loves the weekend!

No one's exactly sure how there came to be seven days in a week. Long ago, it may have been the time between one market day and another, or maybe it was just one-fourth of a moon month. But after all this time, a seven-day week feels just about right.

When is it 13 o'clock?

After 12 o'clock, of course! Clocks that number the hours from 1 to 24 are known as 24-hour clocks. Until noon, the hours are numbered 1 to 12. After noon, you just keep on counting.

The ancient Greeks had a ten-day week. It was a long wait until the weekend!

How long is a minute?

A minute isn't long— it's just enough time to peel an apple! There are 60 seconds in a minute and 60 minutes in an hour. The number 60 was chosen more than 5,000 years ago, probably because so many different numbers go into it evenly.

The first clocks and sundials showed only the hours. Today, people need to know the time to the nearest minute—to catch trains on time, for example!

Why does a watch tick?

More than 20 tiny wheels are packed neatly inside a watch. You can hear them tick and tock as the teeth of one wheel lock into the teeth of the next. The moving wheels keep time and slowly turn the hands around the watch face.

How did people tell time before clocks?

Before clocks were invented, people told time by looking at the Sun. They got up at sunrise and went to bed when it was dark. They ate lunch when the Sun was high up above and ate dinner when it set in the west.

Sailors usually work for four hours at a time. Bells ring every half-hour—one after half an hour, two after an hour, and so on. When eight bells sound, the shift is over, and the sailors can take a well-earned rest.

How does a grandfather keep good time?

A tall grandfather clock has a long pendulum that swings back and forth in a steady rhythm. With every swing, wheels inside the clock slowly turn, moving the hands around the face. Winding the clock with a key stops it from slowing down.

Sundials are one of the oldest kinds of clocks. Instead of a moving hand, they have a shadow cast by the Sun. As Earth turns during the day, the "hand" moves around the clock.

How can you split a second?

Today's electronic timers are so accurate that they can split a second into a million parts. In competitions, athletes are timed to a hundredth of a second—that's less than the time it takes for you to blink.

Which timer was a bunch of old rope?

About 400 years ago, a ship's speed was measured with a log tied to a knotted rope. The sailors threw the log overboard and counted how many knots unwound as the ship moved forward. They used an hourglass to accurately time it. Today, sailors still measure a ship's speed in knots. One knot is just under 1.3 miles per hour (2km/h).

Musicians use noisy clicking timers called metronomes to help them stay in time. Orchestras don't— they have a silent waving conductor!

How can you cook an egg using sand?

Four minutes is all it takes for the sand inside an egg timer to run from the top to the bottom. And that's just the right time to soft-boil an egg. Hourglasses are simple and accurate and have been used for hundreds of years. Once the timer has finished, you just turn it upside down to start again!

Cyclists attach speedometers to the wheels of their bikes to measure how fast they're riding.

What's the time on Earth?

What time it is depends on where you are! At exactly the same moment, clocks around the world tell completely different times. Every country sets its own time so that it's noon when the Sun is highest in the sky. That way, everyone gets up when it's getting light and goes to sleep when it's dark.

Alaska
It's seven o'clock. It's the start of a new day.

Traveling across time zones can confuse your body clock. Air passengers may have breakfast in London, England, fly to New York, and arrive in time for . . . a second breakfast!

New York City
It's noon—time to think about lunch!

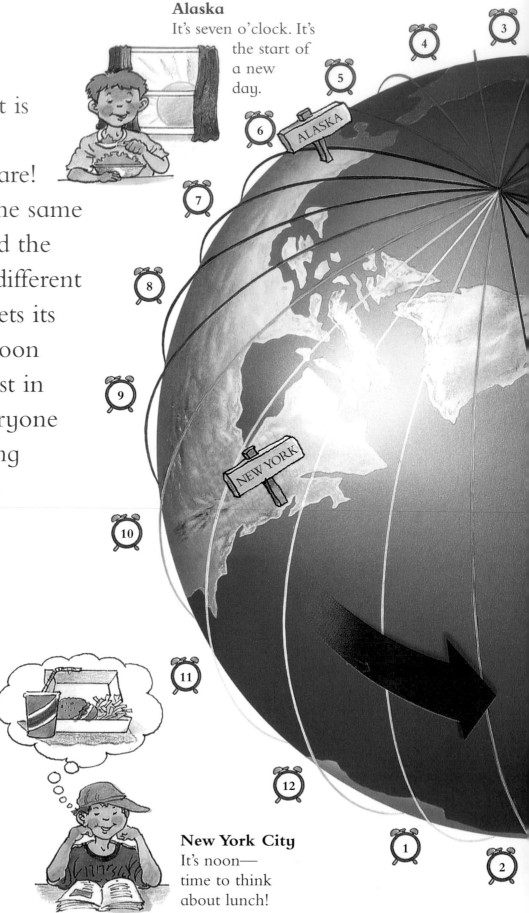

Central Siberia, Russia
It's midnight. The day is over.

To keep track of time, Earth has been split up into 24 slices, like stripes on a beach ball. These are time zones, and there is one zone for each hour of the day. Some big countries have more than one time zone.

What's the time in space?

It must be difficult to tell time when you're in space—a clock won't work, and you can't use the Moon, Earth, or the Sun! Astronauts stay in touch with base and follow a particular Earth time. It's their radio, not their clock, that tells them the time!

Nigeria
It's six o'clock. All the children are home from school.

SIBERIA

NIGERIA

How long does a person live?

Most women live longer than men. The oldest person ever was a woman who lived to be more than 120 years old.

Most of us will live to enjoy about 70 birthdays— as long as we stay fit and healthy. Humans live about the same length of time as elephants, ravens, and some parrots!

King Tutankhamen of Egypt died when he was only 18 years old, but his tomb has survived for more than 3,000 years.

How long does a mayfly live?

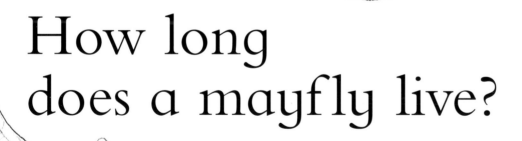

A mayfly lives only for about a day. It unfolds its wings for the first time in the morning and folds them for the last time at night. That's just long enough for mayflies to mate and lay their eggs before they die.

Cats live for about 15 years. Mice live for only two— that's if they're not caught first!

How long does a tree live?

Trees grow very slowly and have long lives. Most trees live for between 100 and 250 years, but some bristlecone pines are more than 4,500 years old. They are some of the oldest living things on Earth.

Trees make new wood every year and leave a telltale ring in their trunk. Counting the rings on a tree stump tells you how old the tree was when it was cut down.

Index